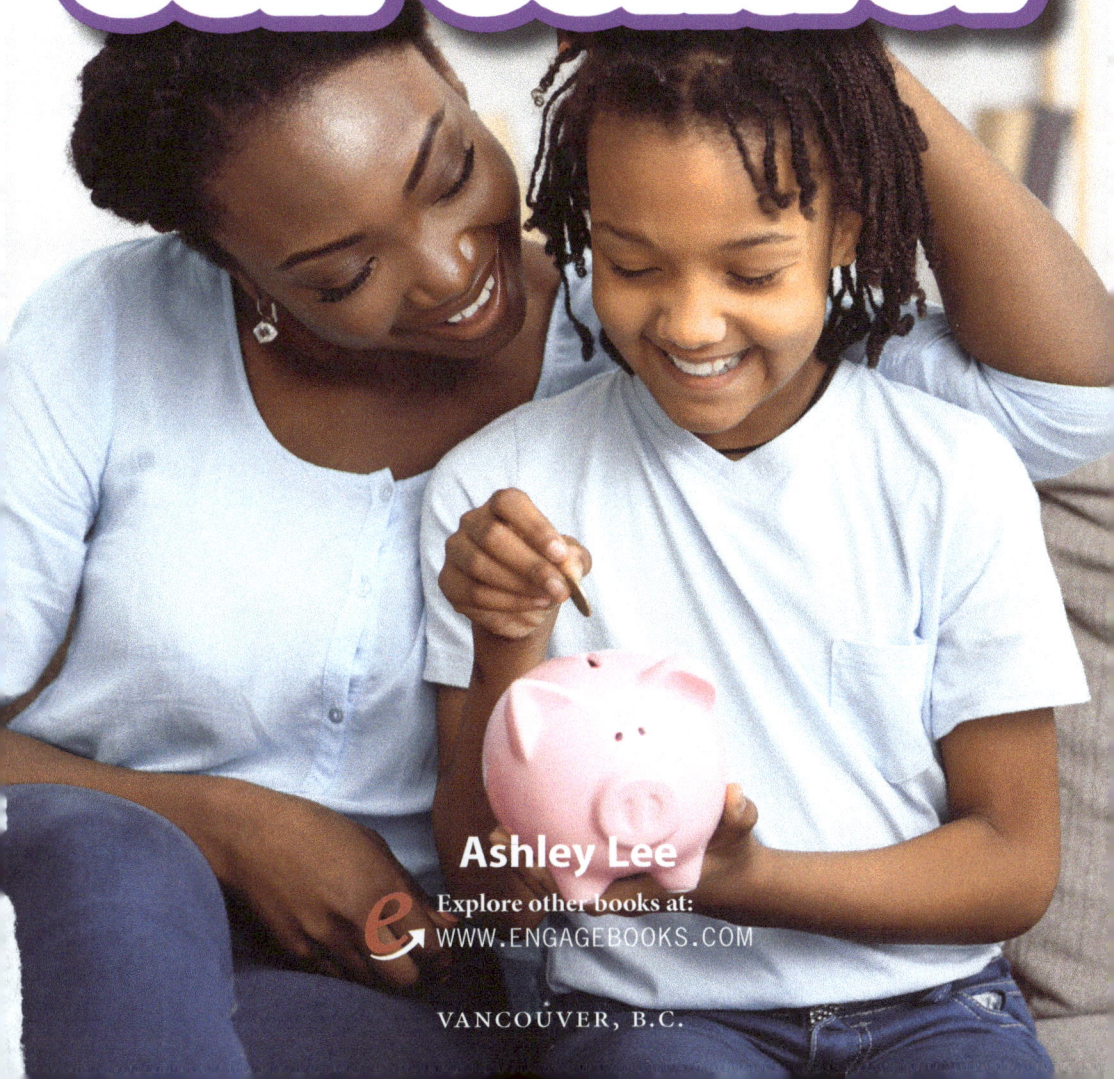

Good Character Traits

Self-Control

Ashley Lee

Explore other books at:
WWW.ENGAGEBOOKS.COM

VANCOUVER, B.C.

e↱ WWW.ENGAGEBOOKS.COM

Self-Control: Good Character Traits
Lee, Ashley, 1995 –
Text © 2025 Engage Books
Design © 2025 Engage Books

Edited by: A.R. Roumanis
Design by: Mandy Christiansen

Text set in Myriad Pro Regular.
Chapter headings set in Anton.

FIRST EDITION / FIRST PRINTING

LIBRARY AND ARCHIVES CANADA CATALOGUING IN PUBLICATION

Title: Self-Control / Ashley Lee.
Names: Lee, Ashley, author.
Description: Series statement: Good Character Traits

ISBN 978-1-77878-727-0 (hardcover)
ISBN 978-1-77878-733-1 (softcover)

This project has been made possible in part
by the Government of Canada.   Canada

Self-Control

Contents

What Is Self-Control?

Self-control means being in control of what you say, do, and feel.

It means not letting your emotions control what you do.

People with self-control stop and think before they do something.

Why Is Self-Control Important?

Self-control helps people make good choices.

It helps stop people from doing things that might not be good for them.

What Does Self-Control Look Like?

People with self-control do not only think about what they want right now.

Test **A+**

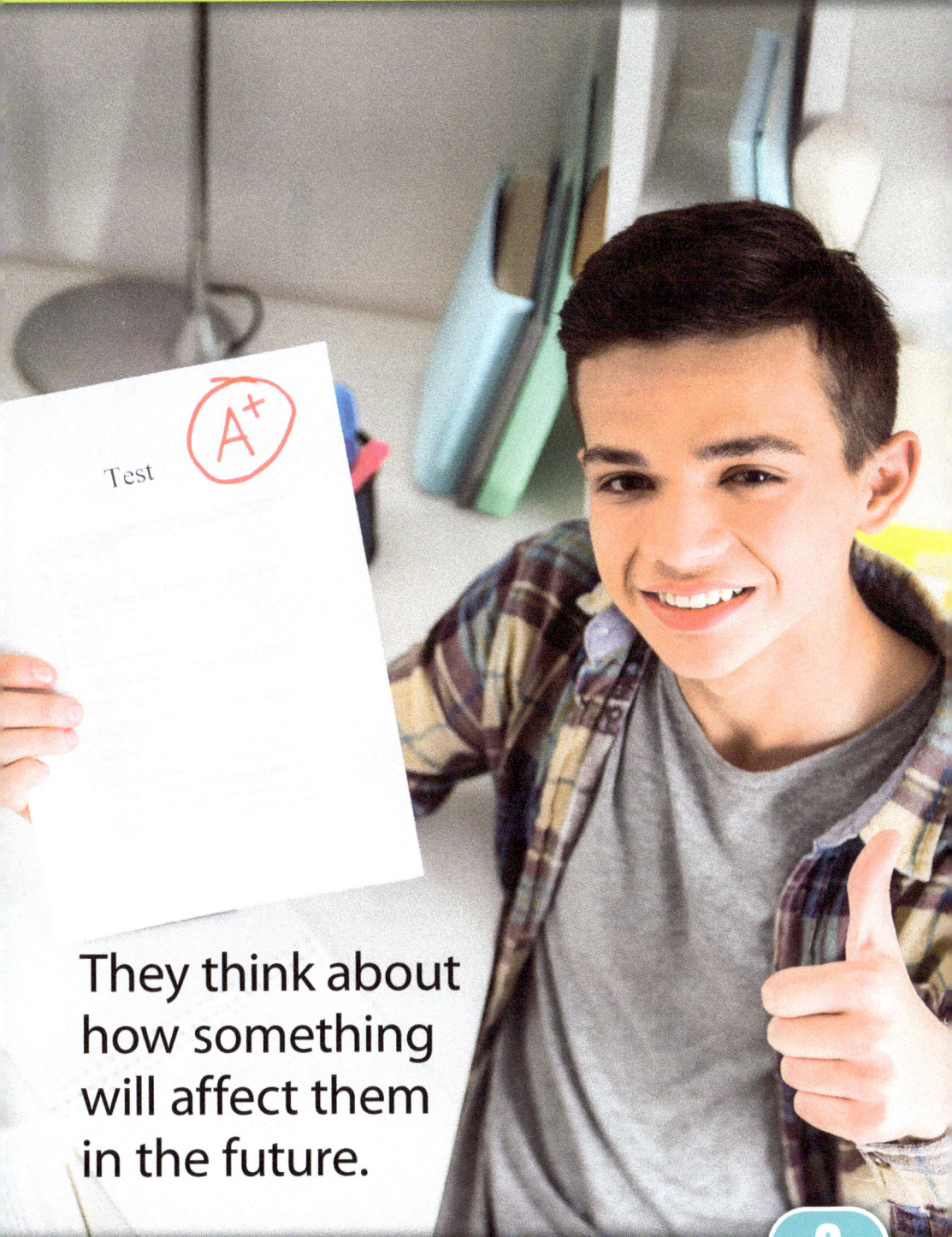

They think about how something will affect them in the future.

How Does Self-Control Affect You?

Self-control helps you control what you are feeling.

This helps you feel happier and less **stressed**.

Key Word

Stressed: when people feel uncomfortable about something that is happening.

How Does Self-Control Affect Others?

Self-control helps you to be kind to others.

Being kind makes people like you and want to be your friend.

Does Everyone Have Self-Control?

Some people have more self-control than others.

People with little self-control can have a hard time controlling their anger.

Everyone can have self-control if they work hard at it.

Is It Bad if You Do Not Have Self-Control?

It is not bad if you do not have self-control all the time.

Making mistakes because you do not have self-control is how you learn.

Does Self-Control Change Over Time?

The amount of self-control you have can go up or down during the day.

People often have more self-control as they get older.

Being tired can make self-control harder.

Is It Hard to Have Self-Control?

It can be hard to have self-control when you want something or are upset.

Practicing self-control makes it easier.

Key Word

Practicing: doing something over and over again to get better at it.

How Can You Learn to Have More Self-Control?

Take a deep breath when you feel upset or really want something.

Think about the **consequences** of your actions before doing something.

Key Word

Consequences: the results or effects of an action.

How Can You Help Others Have More Self-Control?

Show self-control so other people can learn from you.

Help your friends find a quiet place to take a break if they are getting too upset.

How to Have Self-Control Every Day

1. Get lots of sleep.
2. Do not interrupt people.

Key Word

Interrupt: talk when someone else is already talking.

3. Eat healthy foods to keep your brain healthy.

4. Take breaks when you are upset.

Self-Control Around the World

Self-control helps people take care of Earth.

People throw their trash away instead of on the ground.

Quiz

Test your knowledge of self-control by answering the following questions. The questions are based on what you have read in this book. The answers are listed on the bottom of the next page.

1 Does self-control help people make good choices?

2 Do people with self-control only think about what they want right now?

3 Do some people have more self-control than others?

4 Can being tired make self-control harder?

5 Does practicing self-control make it easier?

6 Should you interrupt people?

Explore Other Level 1 Readers.

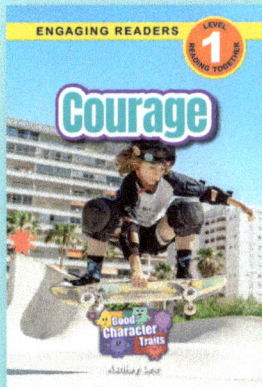

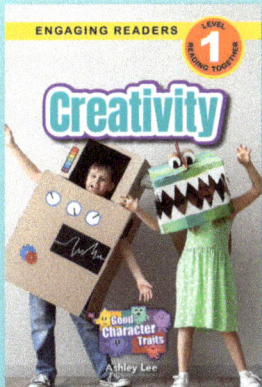

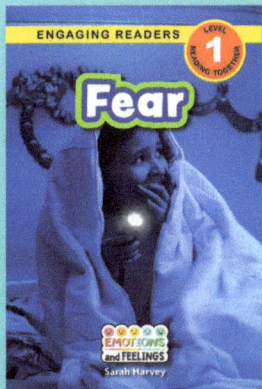

Answers: 1. Yes 2. No 3. Yes 4. Yes 5. Yes 6. No

www.ingramcontent.com/pod-product-compliance
Lightning Source LLC
Chambersburg PA
CBHW052036030426
42337CB00027B/5035